everytime press

School Daze

Poetry-based reading program
for 10 to 13 year olds

with text and illustrations by

Irene Buckler

everytime press

everytime press

Everytime Press
32 Meredith Street
Sefton Park SA 5083
Australia

Email: everytimepress@outlook.com
Website: https://everytimepress.com/
Everytime Press catalogue: https://everytimepress.com/everytime-press-catalogue/

Cover design copyright © Matt Potter
Cover illustrations copyright © Irene Buckler
Author photograph used by permission of the author

Everytime Press is a member of
the Bequem Publishing collective
https://www.bequempublishing.com/

Introduction

I wrote *School Daze* to fulfil a need. I was a teacher-librarian in charge of a library with twenty-five thousand titles on the shelves, none of which could hook my senior primary students into poetry. That is when I decided to write my own poems for them. What began as one or two poems quickly grew into a collection. Students kept asking for more, and so it continued until the poems became a body of work.

School Daze is much more than a stand-alone collection of poems. It is also a narrative that follows the (mis)adventures of its memorable characters in various classroom settings, studying different subjects and participating in sporting events, culminating with the customary awards assembly at the end of the school year. *School Daze* also demonstrates and explains poetic forms, including long poems, short poems, limericks, shape poems, sonnets, acrostic poems and rhyming couplets.

Three decades teaching experience in Australian schools has equipped me with a well-honed understanding of resources and support materials that work best for both students and teachers. Students relate to school stories and if they have outrageous characters doing hilarious things, all the better. Having a nudist, who doesn't like to wear clothes, for a classmate makes for some unusual times. Teachers appreciate programs that engage student interest and come with curriculum-linked teacher resources. *School Daze* suits the needs of students and their teachers.

While *School Daze* offers many opportunities for formal study of language and the poetic form, it also taps into important issues, such as stereotyping, being different, working as a team, growing up, belonging and mateship. Over the course of a school year, the characters mature, bonds strengthen, and in the end, their teacher recognises positives in all. In *School Daze,* everyone can be a winner. Every student deserves a happy ending.

You should know that the *School Daze* poetry and teaching resources have been "road-tested" with actual students in an actual school library. Mrs Bubbler, the teacher-librarian in *School Daze,* is me, but of course, any resemblance of any other character to persons living or dead is completely coincidental. That's my story, anyway.

School Daze hooked my senior primary students into reading and poetry and it can do the same for yours.

Let the *School Daze* begin!

Irene Buckler,
Sydney, Australia,
October 2020

How to Use This Book

School Daze is a self-contained literature-based reading program aimed at 10 to 13 year old students.

A character-driven narrative, the *School Daze* collection follows a group of students from the beginning of one school year to its end. Their story unfolds in a series of long poems, which are interspersed with shorter poems, exemplifying various poetic forms.

The first poem, 'Me and My Pals' (page 10), introduces the characters. The first teaching/learning activities, 'Limericks' (page 64), 'Alliteration' (page 82) and 'Popularity Poll' (page 84), provide the opportunity for students to discuss the characters and to get to know them. These teaching/learning activities also stimulate self-reflection and are a springboard to exploring the class dynamics of your class. Familiarity with the characters will enhance student engagement with all *School Daze* poetry.

While the teaching/learning activities that accompany the *School Daze* poems are language focussed, there is a natural cross over to personal development and health, and visual arts. Teaching/learning activities, such as 'Phobias' (page 88) and 'Characterisations' (page 90) enhance vocabulary development and examine language features, but they also tap into students' issues and experiences at school. As they work through the *School Daze* teaching/learning activities, students will write poems, draw pictures, undertake research, discuss ideas, express opinions, formulate questions, and more.

Teachers may choose to do all, some or a few of the teaching/learning activities. They may modify or add to the teaching/learning activities to suit their purposes. Because each class is different, *School Daze* includes poetic forms that range in difficulty to suit the diverse nature of learners. Most students, for example, will enjoy writing limericks, rhyming couplets or acrostic poems. Very few would appreciate or be able to compose a sonnet.

The poems in *School Daze* should first be read in chronological order. Once the whole story has been told, revisiting personal or class favourites is a natural progression. In my experience, students enjoy hearing their favourite poems over and over.

School Daze is a rich teacher resource book that lends itself to many teaching/ learning opportunities and includes a handy exposition of the features and characteristics of each type of poem in the collection.

Have fun with *School Daze*. Your students will appreciate it.

Contents

Poems are like songs

Although they do not have tunes, they sound good when they are read aloud.

That is why most poems have a certain rhythm and rhyme – and sometimes even a chorus.

School Daze demonstrates various poetic types – some rhyme, some do not – but all will make you smile.

Long Poems

Taken separately, *Me and My Pals, Our Teachers, Lunchtime, Amen, Computer Lab, Library, Fitness, Swimming, Disco* and *Presentation Assembly* are all long (or longish) poems without separate verses.

However, they could also be joined together to make one very long poem, which tells the story of the children and teachers at My School in My Town, Australia.

Short Poems

Short poems need to make their point very quickly. There are lots of short poems in *School Daze*.

Except for *Thirteen*, which is a single verse, the other short poems in *School Daze* show special poetry types.

Limericks

Limericks always have five lines.

The rhyming pattern of the lines is A A B B A – which means that the first, second and last lines rhyme with each other, while the third and fourth lines have a separate rhyme.

The perfect limerick has eight syllables in the first, second and fifth lines, and six syllables in the third and fourth lines.

The exact rhythm and rhyme of the perfect limerick is demonstrated in the nonsense example:

dah dahdah dah dahdah dah dum

dah dahdah dah dahdah dah dum

dahdah dahdah dah dee

dahdah dahdah dah dee

dahdah dahdah dah dahdah dah dum

The limericks in *School Daze* are:

Bevan the Bully	*Sarah the Sneaky*	*Stinky Isabella*
Warren the Whinger	*Hank the Hunk*	*Norman the Nerd*
Liz the Luscious	*Poppy the Pipsqueak*	*Robert the Brave*
Nelson the Nudist	*Marvin the Mean*	*Averill the Absurd*
Freddy the Foolish		

Some of them are not perfect. ☺

Rhyming Couplets

A rhyming couplet is a pair of lines which rhyme.

All of the long poems are written in rhyming couplets, but *The Great (and Not So Great) Moments in School Sport* has twelve short poems, each of which is one rhyming couplet long.

Sonnets

A sonnet is a formal poem.

Sonnets always have fourteen lines, and like *Robert's Sonnet to* Liz, they are often about love.

A sonnet's rhyming pattern is A B A B C D C D E F E F G G – for twelve lines, alternate lines rhyme with each other and the sonnet finishes with a rhyming couplet.

The exact rhythm (iambic pentameter) and rhyme of a perfect sonnet is demonstrated in this nonsense example:

dahdum dahdum dahdum dahdum dahdum

dahdum dahdum dahdum dahdum dahdee

dahdum dahdum dahdum dahdum dahdum

dahdum dahdum dahdum dahdum dahdee

dahdum dahdum dahdum dahdum dahdoh

dahdum dahdum dahdum dahdum dahdoo

dahdum dahdum dahdum dahdum dahdoh

dahdum dahdum dahdum dahdum dahdoo

dahdum dahdum dahdum dahdum dahdit

dahdum dahdum dahdum dahdum dahdat

dahdum dahdum dahdum dahdum dahdit

dahdum dahdum dahdum dahdum dahdat

dahdum dahdum dahdum dahdum dahdow

dahdum dahdum dahdum dahdum dahdow

Acrostic Poems

Acrostic poetry is fun and easy to write. Each line of an acrostic poem begins with a letter of the word, about which the poem is being composed.

My School is an acrostic poem, where each line is a phrase and the lines rhyme.

A Poem with a Chorus

Like a song, *Mondayitis* has a chorus.

Each of its verses ends with Averill singing *Tra la la la* – except the ninth where every one joins in with her.

Monorhymes

A monorhyme is a poem where every line ends with the same rhyme. While strictly speaking, *Music* is not a monorhyme, it does have four verses which demonstrate the form.

Its rhyming pattern is A A A A B B B B C C C C D D D D .

Shape Poems

Shape poems do not have to rhyme, but they must fit exactly into the shape of whatever the poem is being written about. *Ball Games* and *School Bell* are shape poems.

Diamante Poems

A diamante poem is a shape poem, which has seven lines and follows this formula:

1: One word – the subject

2: Two adjectives describing the subject

3: Three '-ing' words about the subject

4: Four more adjectives about the subject

5: Three more '-ing' about the subject

6: Two adjectives

7: Synonym or antonym for the subject

The idea is to end up with a poem that is shaped like a diamond. *Playground* is a diamante poem.

There are many poetic forms. *School Daze* demonstrates just a few.

Back row: Bevan, Marvin, Hank

Middle row: Norman, Averill, Warren,
Nelson, Liz, Robert, Isabella

Front row: Poppy, Freddy, Sarah

The age-old battle between students

and their teachers continues in

School Daze

A Story in Rhyme

Disclaimer

Names have been changed to prevent prosecution.

Please do not attempt to replicate these scenarios in your classroom.

Poems

Me and My Pals

Welcome to My School, in My Town, Australia

And to its collection of weird *animalia*,

Like Bevan the Bully and Stinky Isabella

And Hank the Hunk, a handsome young fella,

Who smiles like an angel, but has very few brains

And Warren the Whinger, who always complains.

Then there's Nelson the Nudist,

Of course, he'd be the rudest,

And there's Poppy the Pipsqueak and Marvin the Mean

Whose tummy's the biggest that anyone's seen

And Sarah the Sneaky and Robert the Brave,

Who loves Liz the Luscious as a beach loves a wave,

Though if Liz really looked and saw how he cared

He might just turn into Robert the Scared.

Unable to pluck up the courage to speak

Such is the strange power of Liz's mystique.

Then there's Freddy the Foolish, a nice little guy,

Who doesn't make sense, and has no idea why

His giggles can often drive us berserk,

When we're busy with our mathematical work.

This brings me to mention young Norman the Nerd

And his twin sister Averill the Truly Absurd,

Who worships the opera, which she sings out of tune

And goes off her rocker when there's a full moon.

Last of all, there is me and I am unique

I have a face full of freckles and a fabulous physique

Without bulging muscles of any kind,

Except where they gather around my behind.

They call me the poet, since I spend so much time

Recording our lives and making them rhyme.

If you'd like to visit and take a good look,

Make yourself comfy and read this book.

Our Teachers

My School's last Boss Head, Mr R.N. Tiegrand

Is a man who became unusually tanned

While attending long meetings in a faraway place

Where talking heads gather to meet face-to-face

To show off their swim suits and smart expertise

Whilst parading around like fat bumblebees.

Here one day and then gone the next.

Mr R.N. Tiegrand had us all perplexed

When he left to become a Big Wig of Schools

And work in Head Office where flattery rules.

Then a new Boss Head was duly appointed:

Miss Ivy Tree, who is double jointed.

With arms and legs so long and elastic

That every stride is just fantastic.

There's no escaping Miss Ivy Tree's grasp

Her athleticism is unsurpassed

All of our teachers try to impress her.

Even Miss Sparkle, the very best dresser

Has swapped her high heels for Nike cross trainers

And keeps her perfumes in sports drink containers

To show how she loves being healthy and fit

Although, in truth, she doesn't like it one bit

And neither does horrible Miss Do-As-I-Say

Whose smile is a vision of bad tooth decay.

Or Mr. B. Jock, an arrogant slob,

Who schemes to take over Miss Ivy Tree's job

With the help of Vice Head, Miss Dottie Bag,

Who always dresses like a dag.

And Mrs Bubbler, who looks after the books,

Throws Miss Tree some disparaging looks

As she speeds past the library in hot pursuit

Of Bevan the bully or some other brute,

Who has broken the rules or somebody's nose

When a playground fight has come to blows.

Mrs Bubbler considers it's really quite odd

How Miss Ivy Tree moves like the Flying Squad

And it is her opinion that the very worst crime

Is when library books aren't returned on time

And so long as the students are reading a lot

It's like giving their brains a booster shot.

At least that's what I reckon she'd say

If you asked as she puts all the books away.

Mind you, Mr Lump, the computer tutor,

Does all he possibly can to refute her

Views on the importance of reading a book

In the modern world, that's all gobbledygook

He insists as he logs on to the internet

Where he does his all banking and places a bet

And tracks down the latest Play Station cheat

Without ever having to leave his seat.

And, therefore, his legs are withered and small

The price he pays for not walking at all

And Miss Ivy Tree has made a decision

To improve Mr Lump's weakened condition.

She's enlisted the help of the school secretary

A sweet-natured lady called Miss Rosemary,

Who summons Mr Lump for technological advice

And he responds because Miss Rosemary's nice.

He's drawn by her voice on the microphone

Though it sounds as deep as a baritone,

Which according to Miss Note, who teaches music

Doesn't mean that Miss Rosemary's sick

But, instead, that she has an unusual talent.

And Mr Lump, who can be very gallant

Brings her throat lollies each day of the week

And listens intently when she starts to speak

As does Mr Broom, who is My School's cleaner,

A man with a sense of smell much keener

Than a bloodhound needs to hunt down a fox.

Mr Broom can detect a mouldy lunch box

From as far away as ninety-nine metres.

So great is his hatred of messy lunch-eaters

That he lurks in the most unusual places

Ready to frighten with horrible faces

All those too lazy to walk to the bin

To deposit their scraps and their papers therein

"Keep it clean," Miss Ivy Tree likes to tell us,

"I don't want to think that our neighbours can smell us!"

And so, it's the job of our hardworking teachers

To tame us and change us from very wild creatures

Into fine young citizens, making them proud

Our heads held high above the crowd

But we've vowed to fight them each step of the way

And when we assemble at the start of the day

The teachers don't know that instead of just playing

We're plotting and scheming, and sometimes okaying

Our plans and our tactics and paraphernalia

To have fun in My School in My Town, Australia

United we stand. We're determined to win

Without further ado, let the school daze begin.

Thirteen

Triskaidekaphobics have made a real blunder,

If they think thirteen is an unlucky number.

Sure, it's odd, but it's also a prime,

A baker's dozen and welcome anytime

Because thirteen is so much more,

Than ten plus two or ten plus four.

Count up my friends and I guarantee,

That they will equal ten plus three.

With thirteen friends, I think I'm rich

And so you'll know which one is which,

They're lurking on the next few pages.

Just take your time: they're not contagious.

Mondayitis

On Monday, our teacher, Miss Do-As-I-Say,

Made us copy our spelling words right away.

No "how do you do?" or a quick "good morning";

Just straight to work with the usual warning.

"Anyone who makes a mistake," she yelled,

As Nelson shivered and Isabella smelled,

"Will write it out – a thousand times!"

So Poppy squeaked and Warren whined,

But Averill sang "Tra la la la!"

"Does anyone have a spare pencil?" asked Liz.

Marvin said no, as he put away his.

Hank shrugged that he had not a clue,

But Robert was thrilled to offer her two.

That was when Bevan pinched Sarah for fun

And Miss Do-As-I-Say threatened everyone,

With detention when Sarah shrieked out in pain.

Even Warren was too shocked to complain

And Averill sang "Tra la la la!"

"No talking!" Miss Do-As-I-Say said,

But she was forgetting about young Fred,

Or Freddy as he prefers to be known,

Who even chatters when he's all alone.

"Yes, Miss," he nodded, but he didn't stop

And Norman leant forward, so he could eavesdrop,

Because Freddy, who never could keep a secret,

Was about to cause another upset,

While Averill sang "Tra la la la!"

"Who needs more time?" Miss Do-As-I-Say asked:

She torments the one, who finishes last,

So we raised our hands all together

And Miss glowered at us like stormy weather,

As Freddy blurted out that Isabella had nits,

Not just on her head, but in her armpits:

So big that she needed them to be sprayed,

With insecticide of industrial grade,

And Averill sang "Tra la la la!"

Miss Do-As-I-Say could not believe her bad luck.

We had abandoned our seats and were running amok.

"Sit down!" she screamed, her hot temper flaring,

As Nelson took off the clothes he was wearing,

To make quite sure he had not been infected,

While Isabella cringed and looked dejected,

As Bevan slapped madly on the top of her head.

"I'll squash those critters, don't worry," he said,

So Averill sang "Tra la la la!"

Miss Do-As-I-Say tapped her desk with a ruler.

The look in her eye was really peculiar.

"Back to work," she said firmly, "And no more chances,

Unless you want to be the one who dances,

With me at the school disco next week,

We'll be face-to-face and cheek-to-cheek."

Well! We returned to our list of spelling words,

Like a frightened flock of humming birds,

While Averil sang "Tra la la la!"

At last our classroom was almost quiet.

We wanted to talk, but were not game to try it.

Even Hank started straining his only brain cell,

A fabulous feat for a boy who can't spell,

And Sarah found her lost spelling book,

When Miss made her go and have a good look,

But the peace was shattered before too long

Because Bevan interrupted Averill's terrible song,

When Averill sang "Tra la la la!"

"Can't you stop?" he growled. "And give it a rest."

Making it sound like an order and not a request,

And even Miss Do-As-I-Say was dumbfounded,

At Bevan's impatience, which was compounded,

By his total lack of consideration,

For poor Averill's operatic fixation.

She skipped a beat and missed a note,

As the tune she was singing stuck in her throat.

So everyone sang "Tra la la la!"

Bevan blushed and sank back in his seat

To hide the discomfort that came with defeat.

But Miss Do-As-I-Say had started to smile,

Showing blackened teeth, which were really vile.

She decided that Bevan would write an essay,

While the rest of us went off to play,

Out under the tree where it was shady.

So Averill bowed like a leading lady

And we left, singing "Tra la la la!"

Lunchtime

Once at lunch, Warren was totally screwed

His tongue was stuck out, all covered with food,

When a big bird poo dropped out of the skies

And he swallowed it, an unwelcome surprise.

He choked and gagged and grabbed at his throat

As he begged us to find an antidote.

"Please," he sobbed, "Get me a drink."

His face had turned from green to pink

But because we were used to his constant whining

We ignored Warren's pleas and continued dining.

Except for Bevan, who was on detention,

Our lunches commanded our full attention.

Marvin was probing the lid of his pie

And Sarah was sucking a salty French fry

Hank was still trying to open his sandwich,

Switching it from hand to hand, which

Did nothing because his food was trapped

Inside a cocoon, so thickly *Gladwrapped*

That he couldn't even see part way through it

At last, he gave in and started to chew it

While Poppy nibbled her Muesli bar

And Liz zipped the peel off her banana

As she smiled at Robert, who sat down beside her

And neither noticed the fat, hairy spider

That crawled into Freddy's abandoned hat

In search of a comfortable habitat

Isabella was eating a chunk of *Cabanossi*

And a piece of onion, white and glossy

The fumes soon stung poor Norman's eyes

While the *Cabanossi* attracted the flies

She laughed at him when he tried to tell her,

So Norman moved away from Isabella

And closer to Warren, who was still feeling queasy

Since digesting bird poo isn't easy.

"You'll be quite okay," said Norman quickly

"Although that poo has made you sickly

Your stomach acid will soon destroy it

And whatever's left will end up in the toilet."

But Warren felt the vomit rising

And Miss Sparkle, who was supervising

Saw he was about to spew

And knew just what she had to do.

Looking around for this or that

She picked up Freddy's battered hat

And thrust it out to catch the chunder

So to be quite fair, it was no wonder

That the spider, hiding under the brim

Tried to save itself and started to swim.

Unfortunately, its eight-legged style

Didn't make Miss Sparkle smile

Instead, she screamed and, pale with terror,

Made a really messy error.

She tossed the hat towards the sky

With little thought for those nearby

Who scattered as the hat was falling

The chunky downpour was appalling.

Miss Do-As-I-Say, coming around the corner

Copped the lot before the kids could warn her.

Dripping with sick, she began to curse

And that was just as things got worse.

One large blob, which was stuck on her chest

Was really the spider, but I'm sure you guessed

That it was there, clinging to her clothes.

It was just surviving, I suppose.

"A spider!" squealed Poppy, pointing at it

And Miss Do-As-I-Say threw a real fit.

Unable to help, Averill was humming

And pleased to see that Bevan was coming

Though last out to lunch, his timing was right

Because Bevan had no fear of a spider bite.

Instead he laughed as he picked up a stick

Which he used to give the spider the flick.

It shot like a bullet, which didn't stop

Until it landed somewhere, in a nearby treetop.

Miss Do-As-I-Say left without delay

To try to wash the smell away

So we finished our lunches, and when the bell rang,

We all went to play, except for Averill who sang.

Playground

Playground
Enormous, busy
Screaming, shouting, yelling
Noisy, boisterous, excited, energetic
Running, jumping, playing
Hot, sunny
Paddock

Amen

For a while, it's goodbye to Miss Do-As-I-Say

On Tuesday, when we all sing and pray

In scripture, as we try to learn about God

With a very nice lady, from the volunteer squad,

Who tells us stories about our religion

Mixed in with some songs and just a smidgeon,

Of preaching about how we should all do our best

So our teachers will realize that they've been blessed

With angels for pupils, all willing and able

Instead of a mob from the Tower of Babel.

At least that's how it's supposed to be

But I have to admit that, unfortunately

My class is well known for its bad behaviour

And the nice visiting lady needs her saviour

Because when Miss Do-As-I-Say isn't supervising

Scripture turns into a noisy uprising

Like the time that Bevan was near Isabella

Waving his arms round, like a propeller

To disperse the pong of her underarm odour

And he hit Poppy's pimple, a shiny exploder,

Which burst there and then, a volcanic eruption

And would not have caused a major disruption

Except that it shot a small missile of pus

Onto Warren's neck and he made such a fuss.

He screamed as if he was wounded and dying.

What made it worse was that Averill was trying

To learn a new hymn and she hummed in the background

And Freddy joined in, which doubled the sound.

Then as Marvin was laughing at Warren's predicament

Sarah removed a pearly white peppermint,

From his bag of lollies, hidden inside his desk.

She licked it and Marvin's growl was grotesque.

"Hey! That's mine!" he cried, but Sarah denied it

"I found it," she said, "And that's why I tried it."

She folded her arms and sucked with defiance.

A provocative move, that almost caused violence

Then Marvin called Sarah a lying sneak

And she said that he was a selfish freak.

The nice scripture lady was appealing for calm

As Marvin grabbed hold of Sarah's thin arm.

Even Robert, who had been gazing at Liz

Could see the nice lady was in a real tizz.

"Settle down," she appealed, and to her surprise

It was suddenly silent, like an early sunrise.

But it wasn't her plea that restored us to order.

Instead, it was Nelson who'd undressed in the corner.

He was *starkers*. That's right: he was totally nude

And the nice lady said he was terribly rude.

"Put something on!" she screamed, covering her eyes,

"And when you're decent, apologize."

But Nelson was puzzled by what she had said,

He thought it over and then shook his head.

"Why should I?" he asked, "When everyone knows

That Adam and Eve didn't have to wear clothes."

The nice lady sat down. She was unable to stand

And it was Norman who stepped in to lend her a hand.

"Watch out! A bee," he called to his friend,

"It's buzzing around, just near your rear end."

Fearing a sting, there was no time to think

And Nelson got dressed in less than a wink.

That was when Miss Do-As-I-Say came back

And saved the nice lady from further attack

After thirty minutes alone with us

The nice lady departed to catch the next bus

Thank goodness. Thank God. I took up my pen.

I wrote only one word, and that was 'Amen'!

Computer Lab

Wednesday morning is really fab

Because we go to the computer lab

With Mr Lump, a real techno-tragic

Who maintains our network as if by magic.

Mr Lump's up-to-date with the latest improvements

Which he implements with graceful movements

From his seat on wheels, gliding here and there

Making minor adjustments with utmost care.

If Mr Lump lets us play games online

We're as quiet as mice and everything's fine

But I have to admit that it's really depressing

When he wants us to practise our word processing.

Let's face it: there's nothing at all exciting

About spending an hour, just basically typing.

So if Mr Lump tells us to open up *Word*

Freddy pretends he hasn't quite heard.

"Which word?" he asks, with a worried frown

"If I can't spell it, can you write it down?"

And Mr Lump explains that *Word*'s a program

Not knowing that Freddy is starting our scam

To sabotage his lesson plan,

With silly questions, all designed

To encourage him to change his mind.

"Sir, why is that my mouse feels sticky?"

Asks Sarah, transferring something icky

From the sole of her shoe onto its underside

A gooey blob, sort of putrified.

And Bevan decides to pull his plug

Then he smiles as he asks, "Sir, is there a bug?

My computer seems to be quite dead."

And as Mr Lump approaches, shaking his head

Marvin yells out, "Well, he can't use mine."

And Bevan snarls back, "That suits me fine!"

Just as Poppy pipes up that her screen is blank

So can she change seats and share with Hank?

Meanwhile Robert confesses to Liz that she rocks

And Nelson takes off his shoes and his socks.

Instead of fingers he starts typing with toes

And Averill starts making a tune with her nose

Until someone complains of a cheesy foot smell

And blames Isabella, who threatens to tell.

Then true to form, Warren is whining

That he's never ever liked underlining

Or changing fonts or typing in bold

Before he asks, "Is anyone cold?

Or is it just me, who's feeling this way

And I should be going to the sick bay?"

He diverts Mr Lump as he gets his permission

While Norman completes a clandestine mission

So that while Mr Lump gets rid of one pest

The truth is revealed when he's back at his desk

And discovers his lesson has been deleted.

Though he's lost the battle, Mr Lump's not defeated

And Norman is sure that he won't crack-up

Because Mr Lump makes a daily back-up

But it'll take a while to restore the file

So he lets us surf online for a while,

Which is what we wanted from the very start

And we welcome Mr Lump's change of heart.

Suddenly we've nothing more to ask

And miraculously, we're all on task

Our computer glitches are all overcome

And even Averill is too busy to hum.

Library

We go to the school library every week

To borrow and learn a new researching technique

From Mrs Bubbler, our teacher-librarian,

Who is very civilized and not a barbarian.

Which is why we copped it the time she saw us

Checking out a rude word in the big thesaurus.

I think it was "bum"! But that doesn't matter

When we were sprung, it was too late to scatter.

Though we tried to pretend she was mistaken,

Mrs Bubbler's impression could not be shaken.

"Here are some questions," she said, scowling,

Her face contorted like twisted towelling,

"And you'll answer them all, the entire bunch –

Or you can stay in, instead of going to lunch."

Mrs Bubbler devised the questions so quickly,

That Hank was confused and Bevan felt sickly.

Warren had no time to make a complaint,

While Poppy and Sarah began to feel faint.

Liz looked to Robert, who squeezed her hand bravely

As Averill sang out, "Here comes the Navy."

Until Mrs Bubbler gave her the death stare

And her song disappeared right into thin air.

Then Freddy giggled, which was totally silly

Because Mrs Bubbler reacted angrily.

She was completely, utterly mad at us

And looked like she was fit to bust,

Which was just when Isabella grinned

And hunkered down to break some wind

Near Marvin who was so horrified

That he held his nose and went cross-eyed.

Then the library smelt like rotten eggs

And goose bumps grew on Nelson's legs

Along the bone of his skinny shin

As the vapour touched his naked skin

And it looked very much like we were doomed

To leave all our lunches, unconsumed.

With little time left at our disposal,

It was Norman who had the best proposal.

"Let's ask *Google*," he said with confidence,

"At times like this, it's common sense."

"And did it work?" I hear you ask.

Was *Google* equal to the task?

You want to know, there is no doubt

And here's the way you can find out:

You'll find our questions down below

So *Google* them and then you'll know.

The questions – exactly as Mrs Bubbler asked them:

Bevan: "What is lucky about the number seven?"

Isabella: "Who invented the umbrella?"

Hank: "Why was it that the Titanic sank?"

Warren: "When does a Scotsman wear a sporran?"

Nelson: "What does a witch write her spells on?"

Poppy: "What sort of disc used to be floppy?"

Marvin: "What tools are used for carving?"

Sarah: "Whereabouts is the Riviera?"

Robert: "Who was the hero in *the Hobbit*?"

Liz: "What makes a soft drink fizz?"

Freddy: "Which famous Roosevelt was a teddy?"

Norman: "Who wrote the Book of Mormon?"

Averill: "What happens at Cape Canaveral?"

G O O D   L U C K

(and remember to use keywords)

Music

"Do, re, mi, fa, so, la, ti, do."

We sing it loud. We sing it low,

Until Averill wants to sing solo

And won't let anyone have a go.

She argues that she does not require

The help of any group or choir,

When the highs she hits are ten times higher,

Than the topmost tip of the tallest spire.

She pouts and frowns when we disagree,

But Miss Note taps her foot impatiently.

"Averill," she warns her angrily,

"It's time to sing in harmony."

Miss Note, who can be so gentle and sweet,

Is sometimes tough, like a slab of concrete.

So, Averill gives up and accepts defeat.

Then we sing together and we sound complete.

Fitness

We always do fitness with Mr Jock.

Last week he ran us around the block.

Taking the lead, he set a fast pace

Which was much more like a sprinting race

Than what is usual for cross-country training

But he said, "Run it hard and no complaining."

Which we did for a hundred metres, or so

And it's not that we're usually cheaters, you know

But fair is fair, and enough is enough.

The task ahead was much too tough.

Bevan and Hank, who were fast on their feet

Had sprinted easily down the street

Leaving the rest of us so far behind

That any comparison is too unkind

And Warren panted, quite out of breath

"Mr Jock will drive me to my death."

But Sarah said, "There's no use sooking

Let's take a shortcut, when he's not looking."

But would that work, you want to know,

Was there a shorter way to go?

Sarah said she knew a path

That would cut the distance, right in half,

And since Mr Jock never did look back

We decided to give her plan a crack.

Poppy and Freddy came along

They didn't think that it was wrong.

Robert and Liz jogged, hand in hand.

Averill thought she had a big brass band

And marched, as if to an invisible drum

Next to Isabella, who was looking glum

After stepping in some doggie doo-doos

Which stuck in the treads of both her shoes.

Her blistered feet were feeling sore.

Marvin wouldn't help her: he just swore

And instead of making conversation

He moved away without hesitation

As Nelson said he felt like flashing

A little skin, instead of dashing

But Norman warned, "I thought you knew

That Isabella has a crush on you,

And if you reveal your hidden charms,

She might just end up in your arms!"

By that time, we were back on course

And Nelson galloped like a frightened horse.

He gave Bevan and Hank a mighty shock,

As he overtook them, and then Mr Jock.

Strangely, when Nelson finished first that day

Someone thought they heard him say

That, perhaps, he might start wearing more

But knowing Nelson, they weren't too sure.

Mr Jock, of course, was quite impressed

Because Nelson's time was a personal best

But you and I know that what Norman said

Had filled poor Nelson's heart with dread.

Escaping Isabella was his sole motivation,

Though Norman's claim had no foundation

And poor Isabella, when she hobbled home

Had broken blisters that made her groan.

We gathered around her and everyone fussed

But we couldn't see Nelson for a cloud of dust!

Robert's Sonnet to Liz

Dear Liz, you are my most sincere desire,

My love for you is more than okee doke,

You are much hotter than a blazing red bushfire,

And I'm a goner like the Sentimental Bloke,

When I see you, it is like I am in heaven,

I forget about my friends and all their games,

I have loved you since I was a lad of seven,

As the carving on the tree trunk now proclaims,

The words say, "Rob 4 Liz" for all to see,

When we hang out as we do at school each day,

And no one is around but you and me,

You smile and look at me as if to say,

Though years go by, our names will never part,

Bound as they are, together by a heart.

Swimming

Australia's a nation of swimming stars,

Our school goes down to the local baths

To learn to swim, and for stroke correction,

But once, according to my recollection,

My class broke every single rule

And was asked to leave the swimming pool.

It was when some lanes had been set aside

For some very old ladies, who exercised

In the water with an aerobics instructor

Who moved her arms like a famous conductor

Of orchestras in symphony halls,

As her ladies used inflated beach balls

In a gently synchronized routine

And none of them had ever seen

A girl as sneaky as Sarah, who took

A beach ball away with an innocent look

Assuming the old ladies would not mind

Or, perhaps, she thought that they were blind

Because they were wearing really thick glasses

And attended oldies' fitness classes

But it wasn't Sarah, who yellowed the water.

It was Isabella and when the lifeguard caught her

He yelled, "Get out, you disgusting creature!

I'm going to report you to your teacher."

But Miss Do-As-I-Say was helping Poppy to float

And Averill was gargling a tune in her throat

When all of a sudden, she started to choke

"Save me!" she sang out like an opera diva

But lifeguard was so angry, he didn't believe her

And although it looked like Averill was sinking

He seemed more concerned about the water stinking

And he glared at Isabella, who struck out for the side

Leaving in her wake a polluted tide

And Bevan, who is such a big beefy bloke

That he has mastered the butterfly stroke

Caught sight of Averill's sea-weedy hair

And grabbed the strap of her wet swimwear

And held her up and whacked her back

She was all saggy, a sodden sack,

But when she recovered, she burst into song,

About how Bevan was clever and strong

And he, poor guy, not used to such praise,

Blushed bright red. His cheeks were ablaze.

He swam away as he caught a *squiz*

Of Robert doing the breaststroke with Liz

Of course, dive-bombing was forbidden

But that part of the sign was completely hidden

By Freddy's towel, which was hanging there

So, Marvin bombed in without a care

And the splash he made was totally awesome

It completely swamped an elderly foursome

In the lanes roped off for their exclusive use.

Their instructor screamed out some bitter abuse

Using words much too rude for me to write here

Although they made her meaning quite clear

And Warren, of course, began to complain

Mistaking Marvin's splash for rain.

He closed his eyes, to wipe them dry

And as he did, a playful Hank

Decided he would play a prank

On Warren, who clearly could not see

Him dive under the water, stealthily

Where he quickly pulled Warren off his feet,

So that his drenching was complete.

We'd already been there most of the morning

When the lifeguard issued his final warning

And embarrassed by his harsh expression

Norman wanted to leave a better impression

But there was really nothing he could do

About Nelson's trunks, which were see-through

And when Nelson decided to swim in the buff

The lifeguard said he'd had enough!

He promptly ordered us to leave the pool,

Get out of his sight and go back to school!

Great (and Not So Great) Moments in School Sport

Bevan discovering that swimming is cool:
A brand-new boss for the local pool.

Isabella dribbling at netball:
A slippery free-for-all.

Hank decked out in cricket whites:
A dazzling sight always delights!

Warren bowled out for a duck:
A sad debut and such bad luck.

Nelson packing down into a scrum:
A tight squeeze for an anonymous bum.

Poppy hitting her first home run,
A mighty feat that's second to none!

Marvin hogging the football:
Another reason for an all-in brawl.

Sarah sneaking from base to base:

A strategic move for a softball ace.

Robert and Liz winning the tennis doubles:

A victory for froth and bubbles!

Freddy kicking the winning goal,

A fruit loop masters ball control.

Averill wielding her hockey stick:

A conductor or a lunatic?

Norman competing just for fun:

A role model for the power of one.

Disco

No one can jive like Miss Ivy Tree

She bends and extends quite effortlessly

Her joints and limbs are unusually loose

And she's never put them to better use

As she competes to be the highest of kickers,

She flashes her most extraordinary knickers.

Striped they are, like a circus tent.

Of course, we peek without her consent

Because if she saw us, she'd blow her top

And all of the dancing would have to stop.

And then Robert and Liz would be wrenched apart,

Which would surely break young Robert's heart

For as they dance, he holds Liz close,

Which you and I might think is gross.

But, hey, instead of throwing up,

Accept that love is part of growing up

And, although, you might agree with Freddy

That they're too young for going steady

There's more than just the one romance

That's blooming at this disco dance.

Averill and Bevan are also an item.

She sings his praises ad infinitum,

Since he saved her at the swimming pool

When she decided he was really cool

And as they bop to the disco beat

If Bevan stomps upon her feet

Averill hums with warm good humour

And Mr Lump confirms the rumour,

That he is smitten with Miss Rosemary

Though, as a couple, they look quite scary

Because, in case you haven't guessed

Our Mr Lump has not been blessed

With the grace or timing or elegance

That one requires to disco dance

His withered legs and barrel chest

Mean that even though he does his best

He hardly moves across the floor

While Miss Rosemary has steps galore

Attracting Mr Jock's admiring glances

And so, he calculates his chances

Of gathering Miss Rosemary into his arms

He targets her with his manly charms

And assumes that she'll be tickled pink

When he targets her with a seductive wink.

But Miss Do-As-I-Say is intersecting

And Mr Jock has no way of correcting

The false impression he has given her.

He gulps as she smiles and starts to purr

Like an alley cat, that's found a fish

Mr Jock becomes her tasty dish

And he, poor man, closes his eyes

As she approaches to claim her prize.

"Let's dance," she croons into his ear

Her blackened teeth fill him with fear

They take their place on the crowded dance floor

As Averill sings out, "Bravo, Encore!"

To Miss Sparkle who's doing the rock and roll

With Miss Dottie Bag, who's out of control,

And Warren's complaining that the music's too fast,

To Poppy, who squeals as she glides past

With Isabella, who sticks out her belly

At Norman, who finds it very smelly.

Sarah and Marvin are hip-hopping together

When Hank cuts in to ask them whether

He can join them to make a threesome,

But Marvin insists that three isn't fun

And he won't share, but Sarah sighs

As she gazes into Hank's blue eyes

Since he's the cutest boy she knows

She abandons Marvin and off she goes,

With Hank, admiring his buffed physique

And soon they're dancing cheek to cheek

Under the giant glittering ball

That makes everything twinkle in the hall

And it's almost time to end the night

When Nelson appears under the spotlight

Where he tries to bare his all, if you please

Yes, Nelson begins his famous strip tease.

Off go his shoes. Off go his socks

He hurls them into the costume box

Off goes his shirt and then it's his slacks

He's already down to his *Underdax*

When Miss Ivy Tree shatters his pride

And delivers a whack to his white backside.

She has hands of steel, I'll have you know

And Nelson blushes from head to toe.

He is not escaping; that much is certain

He gets wrapped up in the plush stage curtain

Where he stays as we finish the disco in style

It's the most fun we've had for a very, long while.

Presentation Assembly

We were standing outside the assembly hall

When Miss Ivy Tree had a sudden fall

She hit the dust, but to our surprise

She bounced back up, before our eyes

Then dusted off her plump backside

And promptly disappeared inside

Leaving us to wait for Miss Do-As-I-Say

To marshal us through the open doorway

And after we'd sung the National Song

Miss Ivy Tree moved the proceedings along

It was time, she announced, to welcome a guest

A certain someone, who was very well dressed

It was Big Wig of Schools, Mr R.N. Tiegrand

And he joined her on stage and shook her hand

As we gave him a smallish round of applause

Since we thought him to be the King of the Bores

Whose speeches should all begin with a warning

That when you listen, you won't stop yawning

Even so, Miss Dottie Bag, sighed

For she longed to be Mr Tiegrand's bride

She admired the cut of his expensive suit

And considered him a handsome brute

Mr Tiegrand was there to present the awards

To worthy pupils, who were working towards

Record scores in their fields of endeavour

In other words, to those who are clever

We expected nothing would come our way

From our class teacher, Miss Do-As-I-Say

But we sat-up straight, cross-legged and keen

As Mr Tiegrand looked down on the scene

Through reading glasses, on the end of his nose

While trying to strike an elegant pose

And when he was asked to get up and speak

Miss Dottie Bag felt her knees go weak

And she said, as he made for the microphone

"Silly boy – you can't do this, all on your own."

Her voice was silky and her heart was a flutter

She was so love-struck that she started to stutter

But Mr Tiegrand nodded that he understood

And agreed with her that her idea was good

"I could use some help," he said, puffing with pride

He called up Miss Sparkle to stand at his side

Miss Bag sat down after being rejected

She slumped in her seat and looked dejected

Her plan had not worked, as she had intended

But in due course, when assembly had ended

She would take revenge on the Big Wig's cutie

And put Miss Sparkle on playground duty

Not for a week, but for forever and a day

She'd teach Miss Sparkle to get out of her way

But Miss Bag had no choice but grin and bear it

As Miss Sparkle enjoyed an extremely rare bit

Of attention from a man, whose main obsession

Was solely confined to his own progression

And even as he called up the very first winner

He imagined himself sitting down to dinner

With the Queen of England in Buckingham Palace

And drinking fine wine from a golden chalice

So he hardly noticed that the name he read out

Belonged to our Bevan, whom he thought a lout

But if that shocked us, we were really perplexed

When Mr Tiegrand announced Isabella's name next

We looked at our teacher, as if to ask why

But Miss Do-As-I-Say had a tear in her eye

It turns out she loved us, despite how it seemed

None of us had guessed from the way that she screamed

When we did something wrong or made a mistake

That Miss Do-As-I-Say would ever give us a break

And that Nelson, Warren, Marvin and Hank

Would get an award, when it wasn't a prank

Or that Poppy, Liz, Robert and Freddy

Would climb the steps, on legs unsteady

To collect their awards from Mr Tiegrand

And touch his amazingly pampered hand

Or that there had been no unspeakable error

That brought Averill, Norman and Sarah

Onto the stage for their moment of fame

It was brilliant, I tell you. We all felt the same

And it certainly proves, (perhaps you have guessed)

That so long as you're always doing your best

No one will ever end up as a failure

When they go to My School in My Town, Australia.

Ball Games

ball games:
soccer, rugby league
or union and Australian rules
footy; scoring points with kicks;
basketball, netball, volleyball and
Newcombeball; throwing accurately
and catching the ball with safe hands;
softball, baseball, T-ball, tennis ball,
any sort of ball at all, to bat or hit
around with friend, on the oval
or on the park, in the light
or after dark. Such fun!
ball games

School Bell

Our

School bell

Clangs at nine o'clock

When it's time to run to class.

We line up at the classroom door

And our teacher frowns as we pass.

We go to our desks and sit up straight

As our teacher checks off every name,

Recording who is here and who is away

Each school day begins the same way

We check homework, then spelling,

Then reading and maths. Oh boy!

Until the bell rings. Such joy!

For recess and playtime

But soon, we are back

Our education stays on track

We are thinking and writing again

Till the school bell announces it's lunch

Then we all eat and play and learn till three

When the school bell clangs to set us free:

Home

Time

My School

My School is a welcoming place

You'll soon have a smile on your face

So many students in endless variations

Creating all sorts of funny situations

Here you play to learn and learn to play

Outside, inside and every which way

Old friends and teachers, together you stand

Liking each other and lending a hand

Teaching from
School Daze

Using outcomes and indicators enables teachers

to provide explicit instruction.

"Poetry = the best words in the best order."

Samuel Taylor Coleridge

However, it is worth remembering that ...

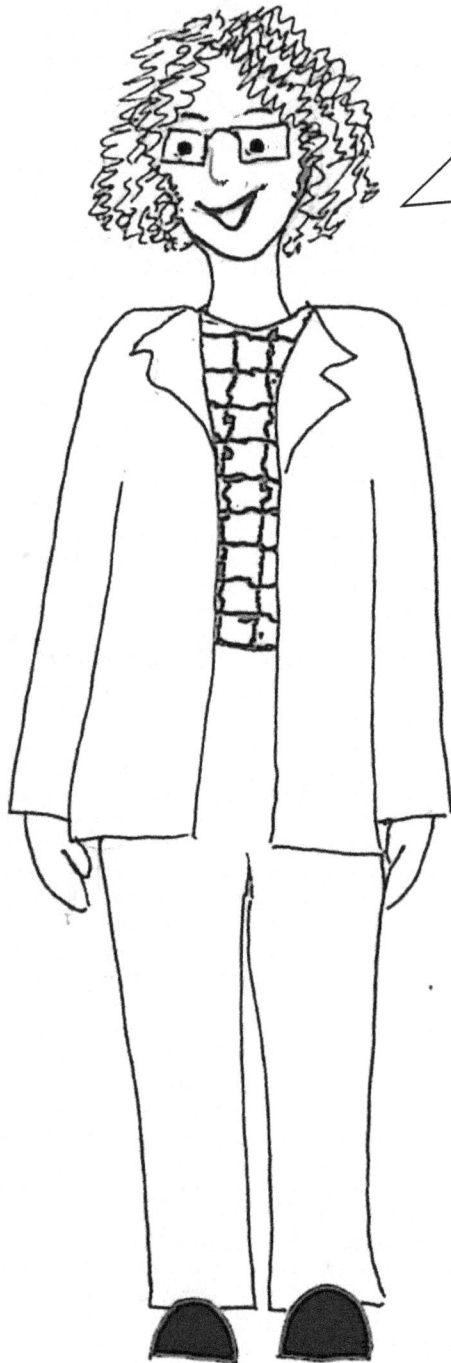

It is not necessary that children understand all words in a poem to enjoy it, but it is good teaching practice to talk about unknown and unusual words encountered.

This way they can enrich students' vocabularies.

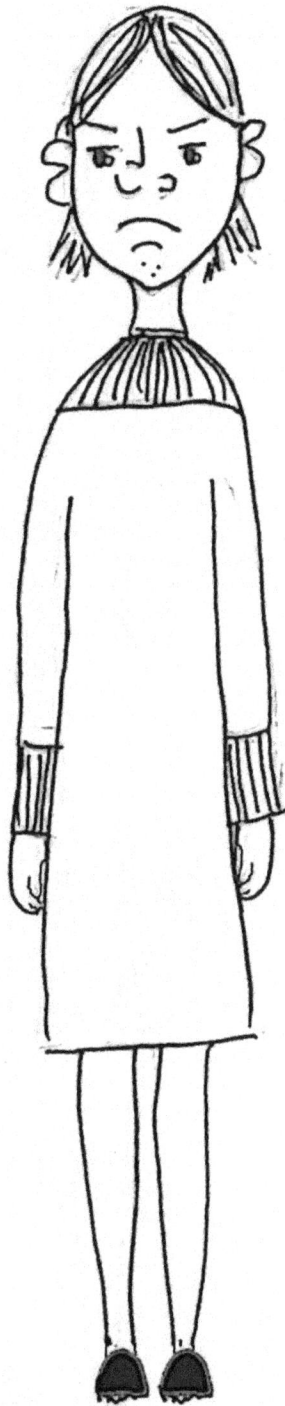

Primarily, poetry is written to be **HEARD**.

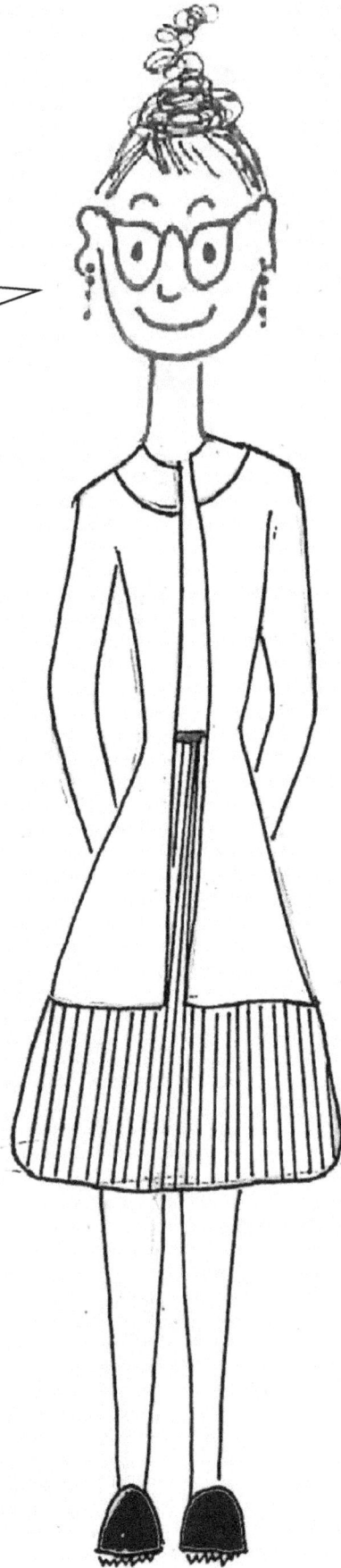

Learning
Activities

including
- **Australian Curriculum Links
  (Outcomes and Indicators)**
- **Learning Experience Instructions**
- **Worksheets, with Answers**

Connections to the Australian Curriculum

Limericks

Outcomes and Indicators	Learning Experiences
Identify the relationship between words, sounds, imagery and language patterns in narratives and poetry such as ballads, limericks and free verse (ACELT1617)	Each *School Daze* character has a limerick and these can be used to teach children about limericks in a number of ways. The limericks may be read as a complete set, or in ones, two or groups. Children may be asked to visualise and illustrate some, all or none of them.
Experiment with text structures and language features and their effects in creating literary texts, (ACELT1800)	1. Read limerick/s aloud. 2. Discuss limerick form (pages 2 and 65). 3. Provide children with hard copy examples. 4. Deconstruct limericks to show elements and correct form: include the beats per line and the rhyming scheme (A A B B A). 5. Consider thumbnail sketches the *School Daze* limericks offer the characters. What sort of impression does a thumbnail sketch give of its subject? 6. Ask children to write limericks and read aloud for each other and to the group or class.

Limericks are written for FUN!

They always have five lines:

Line 1   If there's one boy who really can yell,

Line 2   It's Bevan the bully from hell.

Line 3   When he let's it rip,

Line 4   Better zip up your lip

Line 5   And bid him a hasty farewell

The first two lines of a limerick rhyme with the last line, while the two in the middle rhyme with each other:

When Isabella eats garlic and *cheese*,

Her burps bring you down on your *knees*,

But it's not just the smell

That has no parallel,

It's the way that she scratches her *fleas*

All lines of a limerick are quite short, and a perfect limerick even has the right number of syllables in each line.

Lines 1, 2 and 5 may contain 7 to 10 syllables.

Lines 3 and 4 may contain 5 to 7 syllables.

When| Pop|py| stands| up| straight| and| tall|, (8 syllables)

She's| not| ver|y| stur|dy| at| all|, (8 syllables)

But| when| she| starts| to| speak|, (6 syllables)

It's| a| high|ly|-pitched| squeak|, (6 syllables)

Like| a| mouse| that's| ta| ken| a| fall|. (8 syllables)

65

Connections to the Australian Curriculum

Limericks (Other Activities)

Outcomes and Indicators	Learning Experiences
Use comprehension strategies to interpret and analyse information and ideas, comparing content from a variety of textual sources including media and digital texts (ACELY1713) Develop and apply techniques and processes when making artworks (ACAVAM115)	1. *Google* 'limerick' to determine origin. 2. Find a book of limericks in school library. 3. Draw characters. 4. Compare and discuss the drawings. 5. Model characters faces in clay.

Read the limerick and draw a picture of

Bevan the Bully

BEVAN THE BULLY

If there's one boy who really can yell,

It's Bevan the bully from hell.

When he let's it rip,

Better zip up your lip

And bid him a hasty farewell.

Read the limerick and draw a picture of
Stinky Isabella

STINKY ISABELLA

When Isabella eats garlic and cheese,

Her burps bring you down on your knees,

But it's not just the smell

That has no parallel,

It's the way that she scratches her fleas.

Read the limerick and draw a picture of

Hank the Hunk

HANK THE HUNK

Hank is a hunk, that's for sure.

What other boys have, he has more.

It's just not as simple

As his adorable dimple,

He's gorgeous, right through to his core.

Read the limerick and draw a picture of

Warren the Whinger

WARREN THE WHINGER

Warren the whinger is always forlorn.

Nothing's gone right from the day he was born.

His face is as long

As a sad cowboy's song,

When he finds out his cowgirl has gone.

Read the limerick and draw a picture of
Nelson the Nudist

**(and be sure to find a clever way of covering the bits
that should not be seen ☺)**

NELSON THE NUDIST

Nelson just doesn't like clothes.

It's the way he was born, I suppose.

When he dresses for school,

He's more than just cool:

He's so cold, that one time he froze!

Read the limerick and draw a picture of

Poppy the Pipsqueak

POPPY THE PIPSQUEAK

When Poppy stands up straight and tall,

She's not very sturdy at all,

But when she starts to speak,

It's a highly-pitched squeak,

Like a mouse that's taken a fall.

Read the limerick and draw a picture of

Marvin the Mean

MARVIN THE MEAN

Marvin is mean and he hides all his toys

Because sharing is something he never enjoys.

With his stuff on his shelf,

He sits all by himself,

Far away from the boys he annoys.

Read the limerick and draw a picture of

Sarah the Sneaky

SARAH THE SNEAKY

While Sarah the sneaky seems docile,

She's hiding her actual profile.

She stabs lots of backs

But covers her tracks,

By disguising her ways with a smile.

Read the limerick and draw a picture of

Robert the Brave

ROBERT THE BRAVE

Robert the brave has no fear

Of bullies, that much is clear.

If they single him out,

He gives them a great clout,

While the rest of us stand back and cheer.

Read the limerick and draw a picture of

Liz the Luscious

LIZ THE LUSCIOUS

No one's as luscious as Liz at My School.

The boys look at her and they drool.

From the tips of her toes,

To her cute little nose,

She's a rare and spectacular jewel.

Read the limerick and draw a picture of

Freddy the Foolish

FREDDY THE FOOLISH

When Frederick became known as Freddy,

It was thought he was stable and steady,

But he turned out to be

Too fancy and free,

And loopy, like soggy spaghetti.

Read the limerick and draw a picture of Norman the Nerd

NORMAN THE NERD

Norman's a nerd, but he's also a twin,

One half of a duo, and as smart as a pin.

When it comes to computers,

He knows more than our tutors

And his answers all come from within.

Read the limerick and draw a picture of
Averill the Absurd

AVERILL THE ABSURD

Norm's twin sister Averill's a nutter.

Her thoughts are a terrible clutter.

But whatever she's heard,

She sings out loud like a bird

And for lunch, she prefers peanut butter.

Connections to the Australian Curriculum

Homonyms

Outcomes and Indicators	Learning Experiences
Analyse how text structures and language features work together to meet the purpose of a text (ACELY1711)	**Homonyms and Ambiguity** 1. Discuss title *School Daze*. 2. Note that 'daze' and 'days' are homonyms. 3. Discuss whether the title is deliberately ambiguous. 'Daze' means being in a state of confusion or shock. Is that what school is supposed to be about? 4. What does the title suggest about the content of the collection? *Ambiguity allows for two or more simultaneous interpretations of a word or phrase, action or situation, all of which can be supported by the context of a work.* *Ambiguity can contribute to the effectiveness and richness of a work.*

Homonyms

Complete the pairs/pears:

daze   days

see   ....

scent   ....

air   ....

I'll   ....

bored ....

creek   ....

weather ....

witch ....

hole   ....

wait   ....

lesson ....

suede ....

been   ....

soul   ....

sew   ....

reed   ....

pause ....

meet   ....

What is a homonym?

....

....

....

....

Find more to add to the list:

....

....

....

Choose the correct word:

Eye / I

don't know / no

how Nelson can

bear / bare

two / to / too

be / bee

bear / bare!

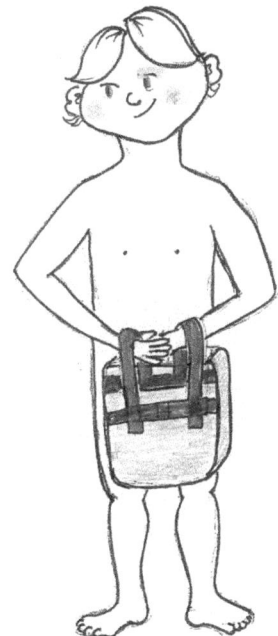

Nelson the Nudist

81

Connections to the Australian Curriculum

Alliteration

Outcomes and Indicators	Learning Experiences
Analyse how text structures and language features work together to meet the purpose of a text (ACELY1711)	1. Children listen as teacher reads the poem 'Me and My Pals' (page 10). 2. 'Me and My Pals' is a narrative poem made up of rhyming couplets – two lines that rhyme. Point out examples. 3. Children listen for names of characters as teacher reads poem again, and write them down. 4. Examples of alliteration are identified and discussed. 5. Children consider why alliteration is used – enhances sound, makes characters easier to remember. 6. Children create character names with alliterative description, e.g. Peter the Puny.

Alliteration

Alliteration happens when the beginning sound of words is purposely repeated in the beginning sounds of words nearby.

In *School Daze* alliteration is used to connect character's names to a descriptor.

Use alliteration to complete these names and descriptors:

Averill the absurd

Bevan the bully

C.................... the cranky

David the ....

Erin the ....

Freddy the foolish

G...................... the greedy

Hank the hunk

Ivan the ....

J...................... the joker

Karen the ....

Liz the luscious

Marvin the mean

Nelson the nudist

Oliver the ....

Poppy the pipsqueak

Q.......................... the quirky

Rex the ....

Sarah the sneaky

T................. the trustworthy

Unwin the ....

V........................ the vast

Warren the whinger

Xena the ....

Y...................... the young

Zoran the ....

Connections to the Australian Curriculum

Popularity Poll

Outcomes and Indicators	Learning Experiences
Investigate how vocabulary choices, including evaluative language can express shades of meaning, feeling and opinion (ACELA1525) Analyse strategies authors use to influence readers (ACELY1801)	**Stereotypes** 1. Consider all *School Daze* characters. 2. Predict which of them would be the most popular students. 3. Rank characters according to probable popularity. 4. Tabulate results as a group. 5. Suggest reasons for popularity/unpopularity. 6. Are stereotypes influential? 7. Discuss what makes boys and girls popular. 8. Examine idea that expectations differ and are sometimes determined by gender.

Popularity Poll

Which *School Daze* character do you think would be the most popular? Which would be the Least Popular? You have 5 votes. Put the number 1 in the box beside your first choice, then number 2 beside your second choice, and so on.

	Most Popular	Least Popular	My Top 5
Averill the Absurd			
Bevan the Bully			
Freddy the Foolish			
Hank the Hunk			
Liz the Luscious			
Marvin the Mean			
Nelson the Nudist			
Norman the Nerd			
Poppy the Pipsqueak			
Robert the Brave			
Sarah the Sneaky			
Stinky Isabella			
Warren the Whinger			

Connections to the Australian Curriculum

Long Poems and Acrostic Poems

Outcomes and Indicators	Learning Experiences
Identify the relationship between words, sounds, imagery and language patterns in narratives and poetry such as ballads, limericks and free verse (ACELT1617)	A long poem is usually a narrative and has no verses. 1. Teacher reads 'Our Teachers' (page 12) to children. 2. Note length and rhyming pattern. 3. Children consider whether the subject matter (teachers) has 'kid' appeal and why. 4. Children examine copy of poem and make a word bank of vocabulary used to describe the teachers. 5. Children use word bank to write an acrostic poem about teachers.

Acrostic Poems

Write an acrostic poem entitled 'Teachers'.

T..

E..

A..

C..

H..

E..

R..

S..

Connections to the Australian Curriculum

Phobias

Outcomes and Indicators	Learning Experiences
Analyse how text structures and language features work together to meet the purpose of a text (ACELY1711) Use comprehension strategies to interpret and analyse information and ideas, comparing content from a variety of textual sources including media and digital texts (ACELY1713)	**Triskaidekaphobics et al** 1. Children listen as teacher reads the poem 'Thirteen' (page 17). 2. Identify rhyming pattern: rhyming couplets. 3. Discuss language and note the ways in which number thirteen is described, e.g. Baker's Dozen. 4. Children research superstitions about number thirteen. 5. Children gather information about common phobias. *'Phobia' can be used as a suffix or as a noun. It comes from Ancient Greek word 'phobos', meaning 'flight'.*

Phobias

A phobia is a fear. Anyone who has **triskaidekaphobia** is afraid of the number 13. Fear of thirteen is a superstition.

Use the internet to find out why the number thirteen is thought to be unlucky. A number of reasons are given. Which do you think is most interesting and why?

....

....

....

....

What do these phobias mean?

agoraphobia ....

hydrophobia ....

claustrophobia ....

arachnophobia ....

microphobia ....

Which phobia does Averill have? ....

Connections to the Australian Curriculum

Characterisations

Outcomes and Indicators	Learning Experiences
Identify the relationship between words, sounds, imagery and language patterns in narratives and poetry such as ballads, limericks and free verse (ACELT1617) Understand how ideas can be expanded and sharpened through careful choice of verbs (ACELA1523)	**Character Development** 1. Discuss meaning of the term 'Mondayitis' (page 18). 2. Children describe their own feelings about Mondays. 3. Teacher reads 'Mondayitis'. 4. Note structure of poem – verses, rhyming pattern and chorus. 5. Discuss the way characters behave and decide whether they are living up to their names. e.g. Does Sarah act in a sneaky way, etc. 6. Teacher re-reads 'Mondayitis' to confirm observations made. 7. Teacher explains how to identify the subjects and verbs in 'Mondayitis'. 8. Referring to a copy of 'Mondayitis', children retrieve subjects and verbs to complete worksheet.

Characterisations

Check out what the *School Daze* gang is doing in 'Mondayitis' and complete the table for each character.

Subject	Verbs
1. Miss Do-As-I Say	made (us), yelled, threatened, said, asked, torments, glowered, screamed, tapped, was forgetting, was dumbfounded, had started to smile, decided
2.	
3.	
4.	
5.	
6.	
7.	
8.	
9.	
10.	
11.	
12.	
13.	
14.	
15.	

Connections to the Australian Curriculum

Narrative Poetry

Outcomes and Indicators	Learning Experiences
Participate in and contribute to discussions, clarifying and interrogating ideas, developing and supporting arguments, sharing and evaluating information, experiences and opinions (ACELY1709)	1. Children listen as teacher reads 'Lunchtime' (page 22). 2. Children examine its structure. As well as being a poem, 'Lunchtime' is a narrative with a beginning, middle and an end to its story (and a complication). Note use of rhyming couplets. 3. Discuss the way the complication was resolved. 4. Ask children to suggest alternative resolutions. 5. Teacher re-reads 'Lunchtime' as children listen and record the various lunch food choices made by the characters on worksheet. 6. Discuss the elements of a healthy lunch.

Making Healthy Choices

After reading 'Lunchtime', write down what Marvin, Sarah, Hank, Poppy, Liz and Isabella are having for lunch. Then rank their choices (using the numbers 1 – 6). Use 1 for the healthiest and work your way through your list until you give the unhealthiest option a 6.

It wasn't me!

Marvin ....

Sarah ....

Hank ....

Poppy ....

Liz ....

Isabella ....

What are you going to have for lunch today – or what did you have?

....

Was it a healthy lunch?   **Yes / No**

Connections to the Australian Curriculum

Diamante Poems

Outcomes and Indicators	Learning Experiences
Create literary texts that adapt or combine aspects of texts students have experienced in innovative ways (ACELT1618) Use a range of software, including word processing programs, learning new functions as required to create texts (ACELY1717)	1. Children examine copy of 'Playground' (page 26) as teacher explains features (page 5, also page 95). 2. Discuss combined effect – visual plus choice of words. 3. List some subjects suitable for describing in a diamante poem. 4. Make word banks of words appropriate to selected subject/s. 5. Children complete worksheet and write a diamante poem. 6. Use a word processing program to present poem for classroom display. 6. Share poems.

Diamante Poems

A diamante poem is a shape poem.

Diamante poems have seven lines and <u>always</u> follow this formula:

Line 1 – One word (the subject)

Line 2 – Two adjectives describing the subject

Line 3 – Three 'ing' words about the subject

Line 4 – Four adjectives describing the subject

Line 5 – Three more 'ing' words about the subject

Line 6 – Two adjectives describing the subject

Line 7 – One synonym or antonym for the subject

Plan your diamante poem here:

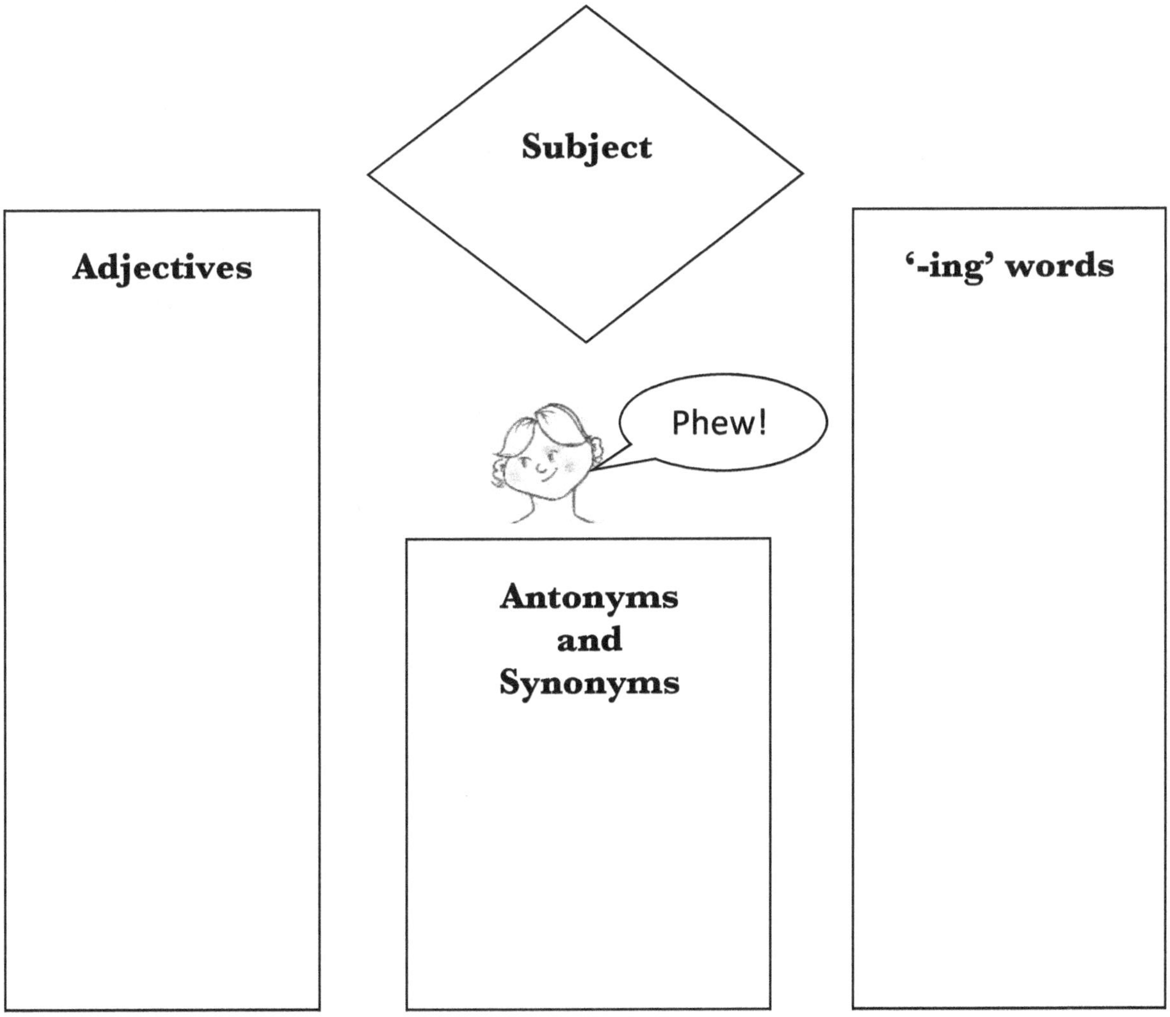

Subject

Adjectives

'-ing' words

Phew!

Antonyms and Synonyms

Connections to the Australian Curriculum

Figurative Language 1

Outcomes and Indicators	Learning Experiences
Identify the relationship between words, sounds, imagery and language patterns in narratives and poetry such as ballads, limericks and free verse (ACELT1617)	1. Read 'Amen' (page 27). 2. Discuss narrative and characterisations e.g. complication is that Nelson undresses in class. Why does Nelson undress? Is his action characteristic? 3. Read again – note examples of alliteration – *Poppy's pimple*. 4. Introduce term 'simile' and point out examples – *like a propeller, as if he was wounded and dying, like an early sunrise*. 5. Introduce term 'metaphor' and point out examples – Poppy's pimple (is) *a shiny exploder* (which had) *a volcanic eruption, each scripture lesson's a noisy uprising*. 6. Close examination and sorting of contrasting imagery – 'War and Peace' worksheet.

War and Peace

In *Amen*, the nice lady from the volunteer squad wants to teach the children about peace and harmony … but the classroom is like a war zone with children out of control and creating chaos.

Sort the words and phrases from *Amen*, and into the two shapes.

Use a dictionary to define the words marked with *.

attack

noisy uprising

saviour   angels

propeller   songs

sing   pray

waving arms

major disruption

wounded and dying

missile	eruption	bad	exploder	predicament*
hymn*	calm	grabbed	silent	preaching*
humming	growl	grotesque*	defiance	early sunrise
violence	screamed	provocative*	fuss	Amen

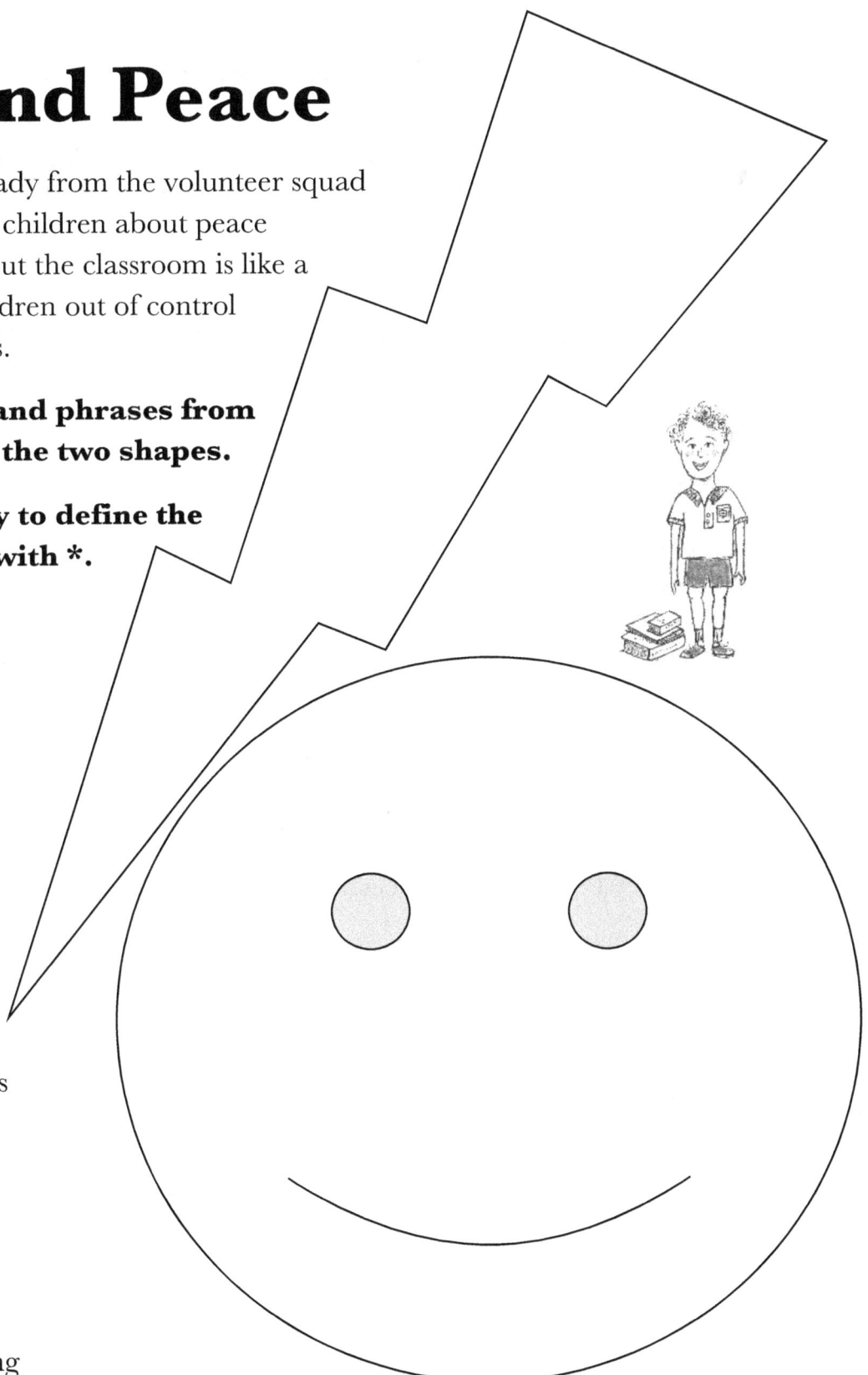

97

Connections to the Australian Curriculum
Characters and Plot

Outcomes and Indicators	Learning Experiences
Identify the relationship between words, sounds, imagery and language patterns in narratives and poetry such as ballads, limericks and free verse (ACELT1617) Analyse how text structures and language features work together to meet the purpose of a text (ACELY1711)	1. Read 'Computer Lab' (page 30). 2. Discuss narrative and roles played by *School Daze* characters. What was their common goal and how did they achieve it? 3. Re-read with attention to language used (jargon)– list all techno-words such as *techno-tragic, network, online, word processing, mouse, 'Word', bug, screen, fonts, bold, typing, underlining, back-up, file*. 4. Consider how using the techno-words engages reader's interest. 5. Practise the conventions of writing direct speech.

Ask a Silly Question

"What's happened to my lesson plan?" wondered Mr Lump, when he returned to his computer to find it was missing.

Rewrite and punctuate the speech bubbles below as direct speech.

Sir, why is it that my mouse feels icky?

Is anyone cold? Or is it just me who's feeling this way?

Which word? If I can't spell it, can you write it down?

Sir, is there a bug?

....

....

....

....

....

Connections to the Australian Curriculum

Information Skills

Outcomes and Indicators	Learning Experiences
Identify the relationship between words, sounds, imagery and language patterns in narratives and poetry such as ballads, limericks and free verse (ACELT1617) Use comprehension strategies to interpret and analyse information and ideas, comparing content from a variety of textual sources including media and digital texts (ACELY1713)	1. Read 'Library' (excluding questions) (page 33). 2. Note examples of alliteration (*twisted towelling*), similes (*like rotten eggs*) and metaphors (*thin air*). 3. Re-read 'Library' and include questions. 4. Note the questions rhyme with the name of the character to whom each is addressed. 5. Discuss use of keywords and search terms. 6. Children research answers to questions posed. *Note that Google will accept the whole question as a search term.*

It's Online Research
or Lunchtime Detention

Nelson, what does a witch write her spells on?

Marvin, what tools are used for carving?

Poppy, what sort of disc is always floppy?

Averill, what happens at Cape Canaveral?

Warren, when does a Scotsman wear a sporran?

Sarah, where is the Riviera?

Hank, why was it that the Titanic sank?

Robert, who was the hero in *The Hobbit*?

Isabella, who invented the umbrella?

Liz, what makes a soft drink fizz?

Bevan, what is lucky about number seven?

Norman, who wrote the book of Mormon?

Freddy, which famous Roosevelt was a teddy?

Yikes! Let's Google it!

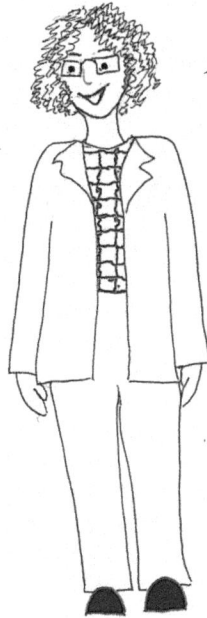

Connections to the Australian Curriculum

Monorhymes

Outcomes and Indicators	Learning Experiences
Identify the relationship between words, sounds, imagery and language patterns in narratives and poetry such as ballads, limericks and free verse (ACELT1617) Experiment with text structures and language features and their effects in creating literary texts, (ACELT1800)	1. Read 'Music' (page 36). 2. Note that the poem has four verses. Each verse has four lines. 3. Children examine copy and identify rhyming pattern. 4. Introduce and explain term 'monorhyme'. 5. Read through example on worksheet. 6. Complete the monorhyme provided. 7. Write own monorhyme.

One Rhyme at a Time

When's lunch? I'm starving!

You might think that it's all <u>baloney</u>,

But Isabella likes cheesy <u>macaroni</u>

With a big bowl of hot <u>minestrone</u>

And lashings of hot <u>pepperoni</u>

All stuffed into fat <u>rigatoni</u>.

No way will she ever be <u>bony</u>!

Finish this monorhyme using words that rhyme with <u>board</u>.

The rain arrived and it really _ _ _ _ _ _ .

But we all cheered loudly as Freddy _ _ _ _ _ _

The goal that broke a long-held _ _ _ _ _ _

And earned our team the sports _ _ _ _ _ .

Write a monorhyme of your own.

Connections to the Australian Curriculum

Similes

Outcomes and Indicators	Learning Experiences
Analyse how text structures and language features work together to meet the purpose of a text (ACELY1711)	**As Fit as a Fiddle** 1. Read 'Fitness' (page 37). 2. Look at language used: *cheaters (cheetahs) – a deliberate ambiguity?* 3. Note alliteration *(too tough, broken blisters)* and similes *(like a sprinting race, like a frightened horse)*. 4. Is it easy to match each character with a simile? Why is that? Does each behave according to 'type'? 5. Match characters with common similes.

Similes

Similes compare two things to make a similarity. Similes start with *like* or *as if* or *as*. The similes below all start with as and some are very well known.

Match these similes to the correct *School Daze* character:

← Sarah is

as wise as an owl
as sly as a fox
as brave as a lion
as strong as a horse
as silly as a goose
as smelly as a skunk
as cute as a button

as plump as a partridge
as crazy as a loon
as naked as a baby
as timid as a mouse
as pretty as a picture
as sour as a lemon

← Poppy is

← Robert is

← Averill is

← Bevan is

← Warren is

← Freddy is

← Isabella is

← Liz is

← Marvin is

← Hank is

← Norman is

← Nelson is

Connections to the Australian Curriculum

Sonnets

Outcomes and Indicators	Learning Experiences
Identify the relationship between words, sounds, imagery and language patterns in narratives and poetry such as ballads, limericks and free verse (ACELT1617) Use comprehension strategies to interpret and analyse information and ideas, comparing content from a variety of textual sources including media and digital texts (ACELY1713)	1. Read 'Robert's Sonnet to Liz' (page 40, also page 107). 2. Reflect on development of both characters: Is Robert's love unrequited? 3. Remind children how to record rhyming patterns using letters of alphabet, e.g. AABB. 4. Children analyse 'Robert's Sonnet to Liz' on worksheet and research origin of sonnet. 5. Discuss theme of 'Robert's Sonnet to Liz' and whether its strictly formal composition (mention iambic pentameter) makes it too old fashioned for today. *In **iambic pentameter** there are ten syllables per line. The first syllable of the line is unstressed, followed by the second syllable which is stressed, and so on until you reach the tenth syllable. (see page 4)*

Sonnets

Robert's Sonnet to Liz

Dear Liz, you are my most sincere desire,

My love for you is more than okee doke,

You are much hotter than a blazing red bushfire,

And I'm a goner like the Sentimental Bloke,

When I see you, it is like I am in heaven,

I forget about my friends and all their games,

I have loved you since I was a lad of seven,

As the carving on the tree trunk now proclaims,

The words say, "Rob 4 Liz" for all to see,

When we hang out as we do at school each day,

And no one is around but you and me,

You smile and look at me as if to say,

Though years go by, our names will never part,

Bound as they are, together by a heart.

1. How many lines are there in this sonnet? ………………..

2. Shade in the last word in each line, but use the same colour for each of these words that rhyme with each other.

3. Describe the rhyming pattern. ……………………………………………

4. What is the origin of the word 'sonnet'? …………………………………

………………………………………………………………………………..

5. What is the theme of 'Robert's Sonnet to Liz'? …………………………

Connections to the Australian Curriculum
Figurative Language 2

Outcomes and Indicators	Learning Experiences
Identify the relationship between words, sounds, imagery and language patterns in narratives and poetry such as ballads, limericks and free verse (ACELT1617)	1. Discuss the rules that normally apply at public swimming pools. Why do such rules apply? 2. Read 'Swimming' (page 41). 3. Compare anti-social behaviour of Sarah, Isabella, Marvin and Nelson with responsible behaviour of Bevan and Norman. 4. Re-read 'Swimming' with close attention to figurative language used. Note: • Alliteration (*saggy, sodden sack*) • Colloquialism (*squiz*) * • Similes (*like a famous conductor*) • Metaphors (*a polluted tide, cheeks ablaze*) 5. Use examples (below) to demonstrate imagery created by figurative language: Simple sentence – *The house was hot.* Plus adjective – *The house was extremely hot* Plus simile – *The house was like a sauna* Plus metaphor – *The house was wrapped in a steamy blanket of air* Plus personification and metaphor – *The house was trapped under a steamy blanket of air.* * use *Macquarie* dictionary to define 'squiz'

Figurative Language

This is easy-squeezy!

Sort these words into three groups.

Alliteration

bad behaviour

like twisted towelling

like rotten eggs

like a propeller

as quiet as mice

like an early sunrise

too tough

Poppy pipes up

blushed bright

burst into song

as if he was wounded and dying

Poppy's pimple was a shiny exploder

each lesson's a noisy uprising

twisted towelling

like a sprinting race

like a frightened horse

cheeks were ablaze

like an opera diva

big brass band

Similes

Metaphors

saggy sodden sack

broken blister

doggie doo-doos

like a famous conductor

beach balls

big beefy bloke

Connections to the Australian Curriculum

Rhyming Couplets

Outcomes and Indicators	Learning Experiences
Analyse how text structures and language features work together to meet the purpose of a text (ACELY1711)	1. Read through the 'Great (and Not So Great) Moments in School Sport' (page 45) – all rhyming couplets. 2. Discuss language used and images they create. For example, Isabella is 'dribbling' in netball. Is she dribbling from her mouth or dribbling the ball (which is against the rules in netball). Similarly, Sarah is renowned for being sneaky, but 'sneaking' between the bases makes her a softball ace. *Two lines that rhyme are a rhyming couplet.*

Rhyming Couplets

Rhyming couplets (as in couples) are two lines of poetry that rhyme:

When you are told what to do by *Miss-Do-As-I-Say*,
You must do what she says and politely *obey*.

With the rhyme at the end of each line given, write a rhyming couplet about Miss Ivy Tree, the principal of My School; Miss Dottie Bag, her deputy; Miss Note, the music teacher; and Mr Broom the cleaner.

Line 1 …………………………………………………...…….....Miss Ivy Tree

Line 2 …………………………………………………………………free

Line 1 …………………………………………………...….Miss Dottie Bag

Line 2 ………………………………………………………………flag

Line 1 ……………………………………………………...….Miss Note

Line 2 ………………………………………………...………coat

Line 1 ……………………………………………….......Mr Broom

Line 2 ……………………………………………………mushroom

Write a rhyming couplet about Mrs Bubbler and Miss Sparkle. Hint: their surnames are not so easy to rhyme, so try starting your couplet with the teacher's name.

Line 1 …………………………………………………………………….

Line 2 …………………………………………………………………….

Line 1 …………………………………………………………………...

Line 2 …………………………………………………………………….

Connections to the Australian Curriculum

Effective Listening

Outcomes and Indicators	Learning Experiences
Analyse how text structures and language features work together to meet the purpose of a text (ACELY1711)	1. Read 'Disco' (page 47). 2. Discuss interrelationships of *School Daze* characters. 3. Read 'Disco' again, noting examples of figurative language such as • Alliteration (*disco dance*) • Similes (*like a circus tent*) • Metaphors (*hands of steel*) • Colloquialisms (*tickled pink*) 4. Children complete worksheet – recalling answers, rather than referring to a copy of poem to find them.

Disco Trivia

1. Two sets of undies were mentioned in 'Disco'. What did each look like and to whom did each belong?

....

2. Who sang Bevan's praises and why?

....

3. Why is it difficult for Mr Lump to dance?

....

4. Who had dance steps galore? ....

5. Explain how Mr Jock became Miss Do-As-I-Say's dance partner.

....

6. Make a list of the different dance styles mentioned in 'Disco'.

....

7. Where did Nelson throw his clothes? ....

8. How did Nelson find out that Miss Ivy Tree has 'hands of steel'?

....

What a little sparkler!

Connections to the Australian Curriculum
Personal Development

Outcomes and Indicators	Learning Experiences
Participate in and contribute to discussions, clarifying and interrogating ideas, developing and supporting arguments, sharing and evaluating information, experiences and opinions (ACELY1709)	1. Read 'Presentation Assembly' (page 52). 2. Discuss what happens in the poem. 3. Compare *School Daze* to own school experiences – e.g. Was Miss Do-As-I-Say's apparent change of mind surprising, or not? 4. Reflect of the way the characters have developed through *School Daze*. e.g. Bevan can be heroic. 5. Examine the cohesion of the *School Daze* gang. Do they respect each other's differences? Recall examples to support observations e.g. when Bevan was ostracised by group for being intolerant of Averill's singing (in 'Mondayitis'). 6. Talk about the characters' strengths and weaknesses. 7. Complete 'Presentation Assembly' worksheet.

Presentation Assembly

It's time to present the awards. Bevan's is done – fill in the rest!

Bevan
Best
LIFE
SAVER

Get me out of here!

Let's get to know each other better.

Isabella

Hank

Poppy

Marvin

Warren

Liz

Nelson

Robert

Freddy

Sarah

Averill

Norman

Connections to the Australian Curriculum

Shape Poems

Outcomes and Indicators	Learning Experiences
Create literary texts that adapt or combine aspects of texts students have experienced in innovative ways (ACELT1618)	Unlike most poetry, a shape poem is best appreciated when it is seen rather than heard. 1. Show and read 'Ball Games' (page 56) and 'School Bell' (page 57). 2. Remind children that shape poems do not have to rhyme, but they must fit exactly into the shape of whatever the poem is being written about. 3. Compile a word and phrase bank relating to a theme. 4. Use words and phrases to construct a shape poem.

Shape Poems

Shape poems do not need to rhyme, but they need to be carefully planned.

Fill the sun and its rays with words that you associate with sunshine and sunny days.

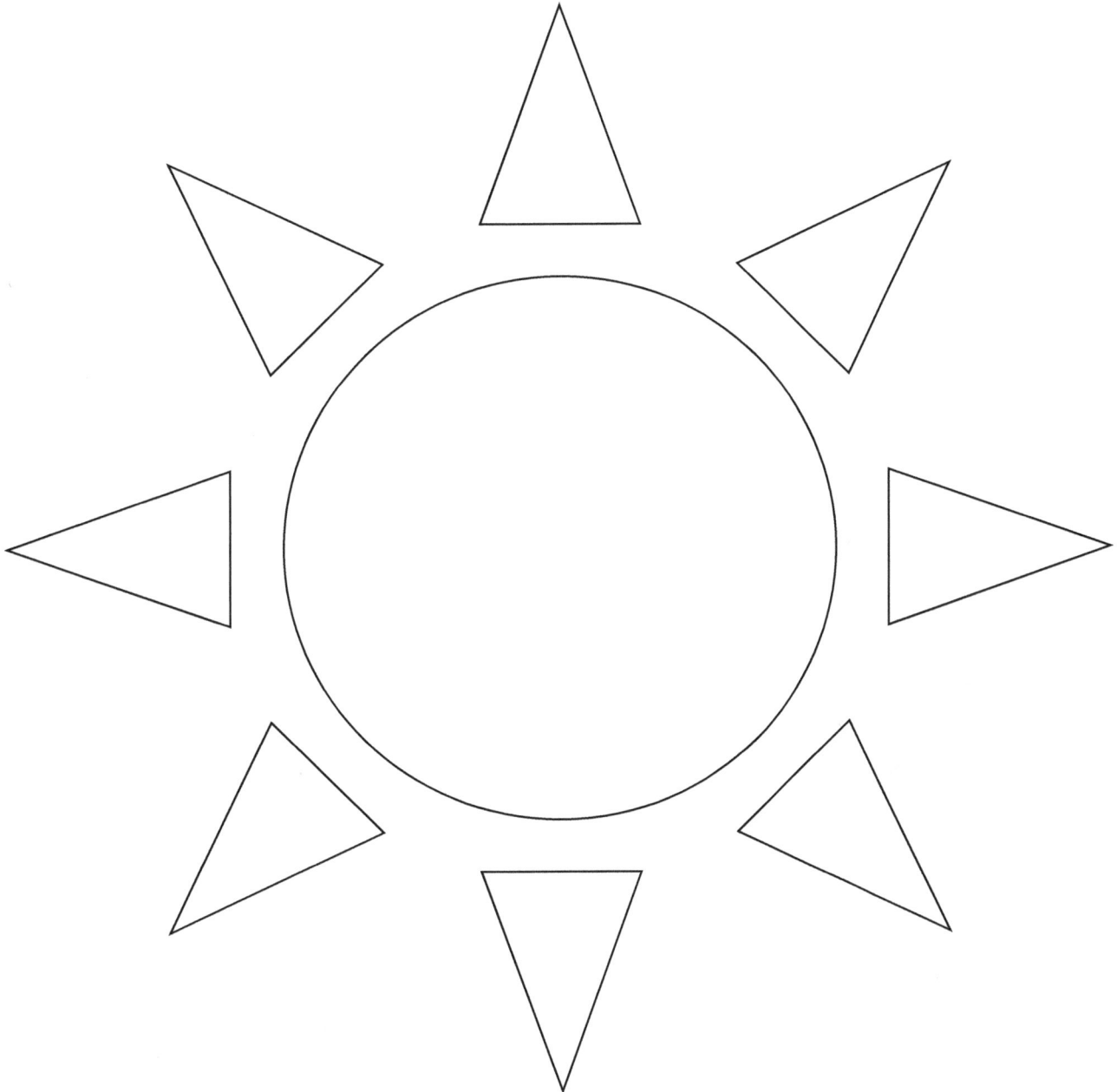

Shape Poems (continued)

Use these sunny words to create a shape poem about the sun in the shape of a circle.

Your Poet

I'm not a good runner and I can't bat a ball.

I can't even do the Australian crawl

But I never get bored

Because I like to record

Every poetic thing I recall.

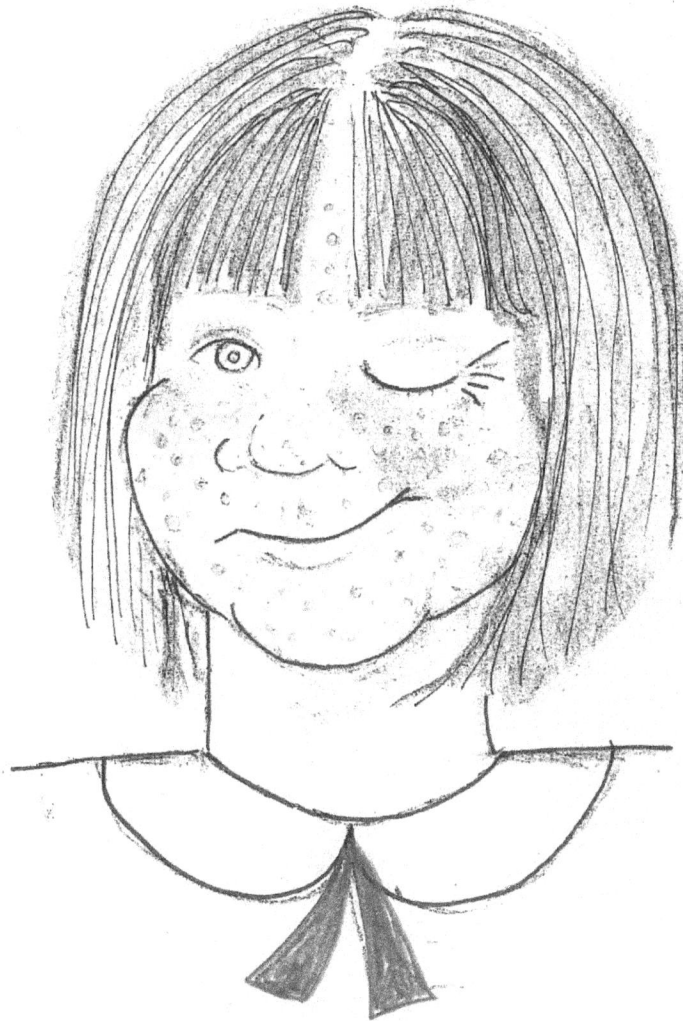

About the Author

Irene Buckler taught in Australian primary schools for three decades. She has been a classroom teacher, a specialist literacy teacher, a teacher-librarian and an assistant principal. Writing or creating teaching programs and resources is an integral part of teaching, and one which Irene has always enjoyed. She has written and illustrated teaching resources for both Blake Education and Herald Education.

In addition, Irene has written many stories for children and poems, which have appeared in publications for teachers and children in the United Kingdom and in Australia.

A flash fiction finalist in "Hysteria" (UK) and "Field of Words" (South Australia) writing competitions, Irene's flash fiction stories may be found in various magazines and anthologies, in print and online. Her story, "Nightfall", was published in *Award Winning Australian Writers 2017* and her collection of flash fiction stories, *Inklings,* was published by Truth Serum Press in 2018.

As an assistant principal of a large school in metropolitan Sydney, Irene was able to draw on extensive teaching experience across all primary grades, with students from pre-school to year 6, from the intellectually gifted to those with special needs and all those who fell somewhere in between.

Irene's approach was (and is) grounded in the belief that no matter the child, the most important factor in learning is always motivation.

If educators can find ways to engage student interest and motivate them, the hard work is done and learning will always follow.

Answers (when definite answers are required)

Homonyms – page 81

Complete the pairs/pears:

see / sea	scent / sent	air / heir	I'll / aisle or isle
bored / board	creek / creak	weather / whether	witch / which
hole / whole	wait / weight	lesson / lessen	suede / swayed
been / bean	soul / sole	sew / so	reed / read
pause / paws	meet / meat or mete		

What is a homonym? A homonym is a word that sounds the same as another word but has a different meaning and different spelling.

The correct sentence is: I don't know how Nelson can bear to be bare!

Phobias – page 89

What do these phobias mean?

agoraphobia: fear of new places or situations

claustrophobia: fear of confined spaces

microphobia: fear of tiny things like germs and microbes

hydrophobia: extreme fear of water

arachnophobia: fear of spiders

Which phobia does Averill have? Averill has arachnophobia.

Characterisations – page 91

Miss Do-As-I-Say made (us), yelled, threatened, said, asked, torments, glowered, screamed, tapped, was forgetting, was dumbfounded, had started to smile, decided.

Nelson shivered, took off (his clothes)

Isabella smelled, cringed, looked (dejected)

Poppy squeaked

Warren whined, was shocked

Averill sang, skipped (a beat), missed (a note), bowed

Liz asked

Marvin said

Hank shrugged, strained (his only brain cell)

Robert was thrilled

Bevan pinched, slapped, interrupted, growled, blushed, sank (in his seat)

Sarah shrieked, found (lost book)

Freddy nodded, didn't stop, blurted (out)

Norman leant (forward), eavesdropped

Everyone raised (their hands), abandoned (their seats), running (amok), returned (to spelling lists), wanted to talk, went off to play, singing

Making Healthy Choices – page 93

Marvin had a meat pie	5	**Sarah** had French fries	6
Hank had a sandwich	1	**Poppy** had a muesli bar	4
Liz had a banana	2	**Isabella** had cabanossi and an onion	3

War and Peace – page 97

☹ War

attack	predicament
noisy uprising	grabbed
propeller	growl
waving arms	grotesque
major disruption	defiance
wounded and dying	violence
missile	screamed
eruption	provocative
bad	fuss
exploder	

☺ Peace

saviour	calm
angels	silent
songs	preaching
sing	humming
pray	early sunrise
hymn	Amen

Definitions:

hymn: a religious song of praise

grotesque: very ugly or distorted

preaching: delivering a sermon or giving moral advice

predicament: a difficult, unpleasant or embarrassing situation

provocative: causing anger or another strong reaction, especially deliberately

Ask a Silly Question – page 99

Sir, why is it that my mouse feels icky?
"Sir, why is it that my mouse feels icky?" asked Sarah.

Is anyone cold? Or is it just me who's feeling this way?
"Is anyone cold?" asked Warren. "Or is it just me who's feeling this way?"

Which word? If I can't spell it, can you write it down?
"Which word?" asked Freddy. "If I can't spell it, can you write it down?"

Sir, is there a bug?
"Sir, is there a bug?" asked Bevan.

Instead of sticking to 'asked', try using different words or phrases, such as 'demanded to know', 'enquired' or 'wondered', to add interest to the text.

It's Online Research – page 101

(noting examples from Learning Experiences 2. on page 100)

Alliteration: twisted towelling, skinny shin

Similes: like twisted towelling, like rotten eggs, like we were doomed

Metaphors: disappeared into thin air

One Rhyme at a Time – page 103

4 rhyming words: poured / scored / record / award

Similes – page 105

Sarah is as sly as a fox.

Robert is as brave as a lion.

Bevan is as strong as a horse.

Freddy is as silly as a goose.

Liz is as pretty as a picture.

Hank is as cute as a button.

Nelson is as naked as a baby.

Poppy is as timid as a mouse.

Averill is as crazy as a loon.

Warren is as sour as a lemon.

Isabella is as smelly as a skunk.

Marvin is as plump as a partridge.

Norman is as wise as an owl.

Sonnets – page 107

1. fourteen

3. A B A B C D C D E F E F G G

4. The word "sonnet" comes from the Italian "sonetto", meaning "little song."

5. The overarching theme of most sonnets is love. Robert's Sonnet to Liz is no exception. It is a declaration of his love.

Figurative Language – page 109

Alliteration: bad behaviour, too tough, Poppy pipes up, blushed bright, Poppy's pimple, twisted towelling, saggy sodden sack, big brass band, broken blister, doggy doo-doos, beach balls, big beefy bloke

Similes: like twisted towelling, like rotten eggs, like a propeller, as quiet as a mouse, like an early sunrise, as if he was wounded and dying, like a sprinting race, like a frightened horse, like an opera diva, like a famous conductor

Metaphors: burst into song, Poppy's pimple was a shiny exploder, each lesson's a noisy uprising, cheeks were ablaze

Disco Trivia – page 113

1. Miss Ivy Tree wears extraordinary knickers striped like a circus tent. Nelson is wearing Underdax.

2. Averill sings Bevan's praises because "he saved her at the swimming pool".

3. Mr Lump has no grace, timing or elegance, which in addition to his withered legs makes it difficult for him to dance.

4. Miss Rosemary has dance steps galore.

5. Mr Jock wants to dance with Miss Rosemary. However, when he winks in her direction, it is Miss-Do-As-Say who accepts his implied invitation to dance and he is unable to refuse her.

6. Disco dancing, bop, rock and roll and hip-hop.

7. Nelson throws his clothes into the costume box.

8. Nelson discovers Miss Ivy Tree has hands of steel when she whacks him on his "white backside".

Also from Everytime Press

ESL Teaching and How-to books

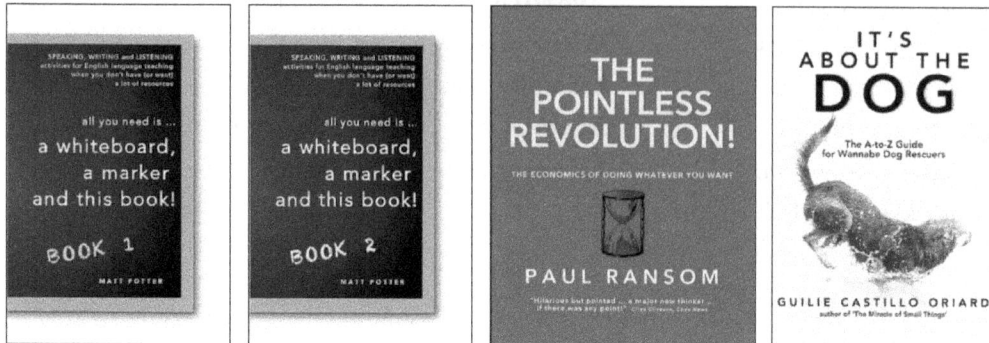

- all you need is … a whiteboard, a marker and this book!
  by Matt Potter 978-1-925101-82-9 (Book 1) 978-1-925101-96-6 (Book 2)
- The Pointless Revolution! by Paul Ransom
  978-1-925536-74-4 (paperback) 978-1-925536-75-1 (eBook)
- It's About the Dog by Guilie Castillo Oriard
  978-1-925536-19-5 (paperback) 978-1-925536-20-1 (eBook)

Travel and Memoir

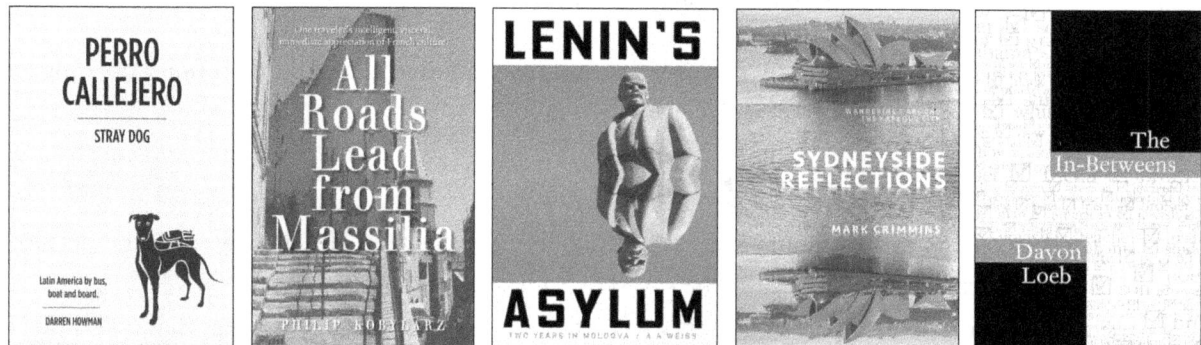

- Perro Callejero by Darren Howman
  978-1-925536-96-6 (paperback) 978-1-925536-97-3 (eBook)
- All Roads Lead from Massilia by Philip Kobylarz
  978-1-925536-27-0 (paperback) 978-1-925536-28-7 (eBook)
- Lenin's Asylum by A. A. Weiss
  978-1-925536-50-8 (paperback) 978-1-925536-51-5 (eBook)
- Sydneyside Reflections by Mark Crimmins
  978-1-925536-07-2 (paperback) 978-1-925536-08-9 (eBook)
- The In-Betweens by Davon Loeb
  978-1-925536-56-0 (paperback) 978-1-925536-57-7 (eBook)

www.ingramcontent.com/pod-product-compliance
Lightning Source LLC
Chambersburg PA
CBHW080858090426
42737CB00016B/2990